Fire Safety

by Peggy Pancella

Heinemann Library
Chicago, Illinois

Customer Service 888-454-2279
Visit our website at www.heinemannlibrary.com

Designed by Heinemann Library
Page layout by Roslyn Broder
Printed and bound in China by South China Printing Co. Ltd.

09 08 07 06
10 9 8 7 6 5 4 3 2

Library of Congress Cataloging-in-Publication Data
Pancella, Peggy.
  Fire safety / Peggy Pancella.
      v. cm. -- (Be safe!)
  Includes index.
  Contents: What is safety? -- Good fires and bad fires -- Fire starters -- Kitchen safety -- Other fires -- Stop, drop and roll -- Smoke detectors -- Make a plan -- Fire drill! -- Getting out safely -- Be smart around smoke -- Call for help -- Firefighters can help -- Safety tips.
  ISBN 1-4034-4931-7 (hardcover) -- ISBN 1-4034-4940-6 (pbk.)

  1. Fire prevention--Juvenile literature. 2. Fire protection engineering--Juvenile literature. [1. Fire prevention. 2. Safety.] I. Title.
  TH9148.P27 2004
  613.6--dc22

                                    2003024063

Acknowledgments
The author and publisher are grateful to the following for permission to reproduce copyright material:
Cover photograph by Robert Lifson/Heinemann Library
p. 4 Tom Stewart/Corbis; p. 5 Craig Tuttle/Corbis; p. 6 Alan Oddie/PhotoEdit, Inc.; p. 7 Spencer Grant/PhotoEdit, Inc.; pp. 8, 10, 11, 12, 14, 15, 16, 17, 18, 19, 20, 21, 22, 23, 24, 25, 26 Robert Lifson/Heinemann Library; pp. 9, 29 Corbis; p. 13 Michael Newman/Photo Edit, Inc.; p. 27 Robert Brenner/PhotoEdit, Inc.; p. 28 Billy E. Barnes/Photo Edit, Inc.

Every effort has been made to contact copyright holders of any material reproduced in this book. Any omissions will be rectified in subsequent printings if notice is given to the publisher.

Contents

Some words are shown in bold, **like this.** You can find out what they mean by looking in the glossary.

What Is Safety?

It is important for everyone to stay safe. Being safe means keeping out of danger. It means staying away from things or people that could hurt you.

Safety is important in everything you do. You need to be extra careful when you are near fire. Fire can hurt you or put you in danger. Learning some rules about fire can help you stay safe.

Good Fires and Bad Fires

Some fires are very helpful. Fire can cook our food, heat our homes, and give us light. Good fires are usually controlled in a small place.

Sometimes a fire burns out of control. This kind of fire is very dangerous. It can spread quickly, burning up homes, cars, or even a whole forest!

Fire Starters

Different objects can start fires. Many homes have matches or lighters. These things are not toys. If you see them, do not touch them. Tell an adult what you found.

Candles, cigarettes, and heaters can start fires if they are left burning or turned on when no one is paying attention. Only adults should handle dangerous objects like these.

Kitchen Safety

Many house fires start in kitchens. Stoves, ovens, and other **appliances** cook food, but their heat makes them dangerous. Never use these alone. Always ask an adult to help you.

If you help in the kitchen, keep your clothing and hair away from the flames on the stove. Do not run or play in the kitchen when an adult is cooking.

Other Fires

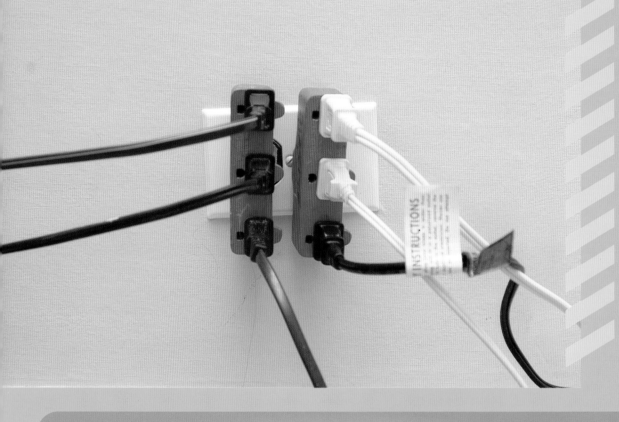

Electricity causes some house fires. If too many cords are plugged into an **outlet,** it can get too hot and start a fire. Putting cords where people can trip is also unsafe. Never use cracked or broken cords.

Outdoor fires can also be dangerous.
Grills and campfires can cook food, but
you could get burned if you get too close.
An adult should handle the cooking and
put out the fire before going indoors.

Stop, Drop, and Roll

If fire touches you, do not run. That will make the fire burn stronger. Instead, you should stop, drop, and roll. Stop where you are and drop to the floor.

Lie flat and cover your face with your hands. Roll across the floor until the flames are out. Practicing these steps will help you to be ready if there is a real fire.

Smoke Detectors

Smoke detectors can warn people of a fire. When detectors sense smoke, they make a loud beeping noise. Homes need smoke detectors near bedrooms and on every floor of the house.

Smoke detectors work best on ceilings or high on walls because smoke rises. Adults should clean and test smoke detectors each month and replace the batteries twice a year.

Make a Plan

Your family can make a plan to get out if your home catches fire. Draw a map of your home. Show every room and all the doors and windows.

Write down two ways to escape from each room. Also pick a place to meet outside. Your family can gather at a tree, gate, or other spot after you leave the house.

Fire Drill!

After your family makes an escape plan, practice it together. Test all the **routes** to get out. Remember to keep important escape routes, such as the stairs, clear.

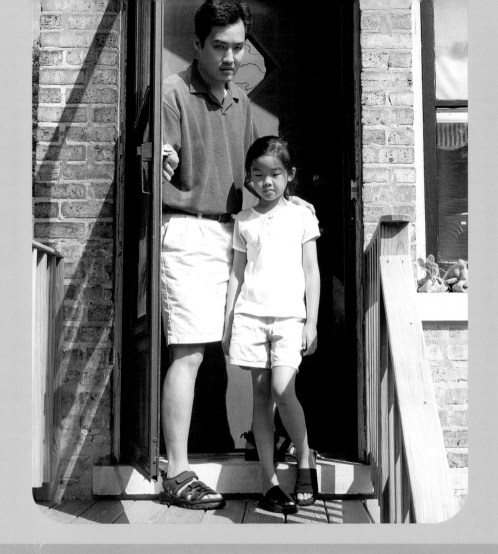

Practice your plan often. Try it in the day and at night because things look different in the dark. Always gather at the special meeting place you chose.

Getting Out Safely

If you hear a **smoke detector** or notice a fire, act quickly. Crawl to the door and feel it with the back of your hand. If the door is cool, open it carefully and follow your escape **route**.

If the door feels hot, leave it closed. If a window is very close to the ground, climb out. If not, shout and signal for help. Do not hide or take anything with you.

Use a window that *is* low to the ground to leave a room only *if* there *is* no other safe way to get out.

Be Smart Around Smoke

Fires make lots of smoke. Smoke is just as dangerous as flames are. It is hard to breathe and has **poisonous gases.** Those are dangerous things in the air that can hurt or kill you if you breathe them in.

Poisonous gases can make you feel sick or **confused.** Smoke rises, so air near the floor is clearest. Drop down and crawl on your hands and knees. Put a wet cloth over your mouth and nose to breathe more easily.

Call for Help

Once you are outside, one person should use a neighbor's phone or cell phone to call **911**. Tell the **dispatcher** your address so the firefighters will know where to go.

Wait in your meeting place until help comes. Never go back into the house for any reason. If people are trapped inside, tell the firefighters.

Firefighters and Other Helpers

Firefighters put out fires and rescue people and pets. Firefighters wear scary-looking masks, but they are really helpful people. Do not be afraid or hide from a firefighter.

Other workers can help if there is
a fire. Police can get people to safety.
Emergency medical workers can treat
some burns or take badly hurt people
to the hospital.

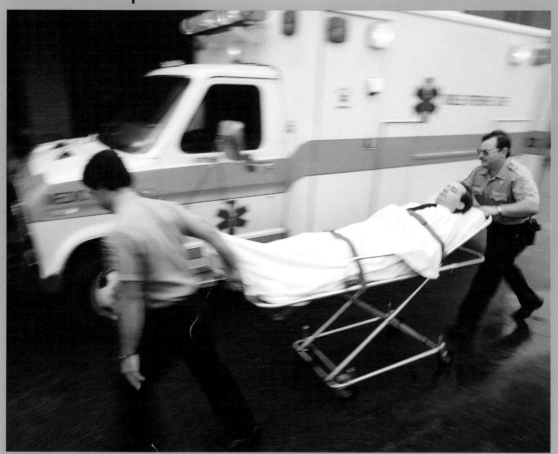

Safety Tips

- All fires are dangerous. Do not hide—get outside!

- Be safe around smoke. Stay low and go!

- Learn your escape plan and teach it to anyone who cares for you at home, such as babysitters.

- Keep a flashlight near your bed in case you have to escape in the dark.

- Hang a list of **emergency** numbers near every telephone.

- Adults can use **fire extinguishers** to put out some small fires.

Glossary

911 phone number to dial in an emergency

appliance piece of household equipment

confused mixed up

dispatcher person who answers 911 calls and sends help

electricity natural force that makes power

emergency sudden event that makes you act quickly

fire extinguisher container filled with special liquid to spray onto a small fire

medical worker person who helps when people are hurt or sick

outlet place to plug cord to get power

route path or way to go

smoke detector fire alarm that goes off when it senses smoke

Index